the PET -to- GET

FERRET

ROB COLSON

WAYLAND

First published in 2014 by Wayland
Copyright © Wayland 2014

Wayland
338 Euston Road
London NW1 3BH

Wayland Australia
Level 17/207 Kent Street
Sydney, NSW 2000

Editor: Annabel Stones

Produced for Wayland by
Tall Tree Ltd
Consultant: Victoria Hall

A cataloguing record for this title is
available at the British Library.

ISBN 978 0 7502 8292 5

Dewey number: 636.9'76628-dc23

10 9 8 7 6 5 4 3 2 1

Printed in China

Wayland is a division of Hachette Children's
Books, an Hachette UK company
www.hachette.co.uk

The publisher would would like to thank the following for
their kind permission to reproduce their photographs:

Key: (t) top; (c) centre; (b) bottom; (l) left; (r) right
(Shutterstock.com unless stated otherwise)
Front cover: Adam Goss/Dreamstime; Back cover: Eric
Isselee; 1 Eric Isselee, 2 VitCom Photo; 4–5 Juniors
Bildarchiv GmbH/Alamy; 6l 67photo/Alamy; 7b Brandi
Pierce/Dreamstime.com; 7t Eric Isselee; 8b Franco-
Burgundian/Getty; 9c Michael Rose/Alamy; 9br Maslov
Dmitry; 10b PetStockBoys/Alamy; 10c Gila R. Todd; 11 Gila
R. Todd; 12 Stephan Morris; 13 Zhiltsov Alexandr; 14
Eurobanks; 15t Mientje80/Dreamtime.com; 15b Radka
Tesarova; 16 Christian Baloga/Alamy; 17t Dauma/
Dreamstime.com; 17b Tatjana Kabanova; 18 Kuricheva
Ekaterina; 19c Marina Jay; 19t Erlendaarke; 20b Igor
Boldyrev; 20–21 Jagodka; 21t Couperfield; 22l Jagodka;
22b nanka; 23bl IrinaK; 23bc
Jagodka; 23br Jagodka; 23t
Paul Doyle/Alamy; 24 Paul
Gapper/Alamy; 24–25
Barbara Jack; 25t Brandi
Pierce; 26 Anton Gvozdikov;
27 Africa Studio; 28 Rashid
Valitov; 29t Radka Tesarova;
29b Denis Kukareko; 30tl
nanka; 30tcl Jagodka; 30tcr
Jagodka; 30tr IrinaK; 30b
Eric Isselee

CONTENTS

IS A FERRET FOR YOU?

Ferrets are small **mammals** with big personalities. They have bundles of energy, and a habit of getting into mischief! If you have the time to give them the attention they need, you'll love keeping ferrets.

ANNUAL MOULT

Every autumn, ferrets grow warm, thick fur for winter. In spring, they lose their winter coat and grow a slick new one for summer. This process is called moulting, and it can happen very quickly. One spring morning, you may wake up to find your ferret has lost all its winter fur overnight!

WHAT ARE FERRETS?

A ferret is a **domesticated** animal, like domestic cats and dogs. This means that ferrets do not live in the wild. They were bred by humans more than 2,000 years ago to help them with hunting. Ferrets are **descended** from the wild European polecat, and are closely related to weasels, stoats and otters.

Ferrets love playing with their owners and also with one another.

Ferrets love the company of other ferrets, and spend a lot of their time playing with each other. If you can, choose to keep two together.

THINK FIRST

Before buying a ferret, discuss it with your family and carefully weigh up the pros and cons.

PROS
- They are very affectionate and love people.
- You can take them for walks and enter them into competitions.
- They are naturally clean.

CONS
- They produce a stinking smell when scared.
- You must spend time playing with them every day.
- You must clean their cage regularly.

CHOOSING YOUR FERRET

You should only buy ferrets from a registered breeder or a rescue centre. Ferrets are highly social animals that need playmates, so normally you should buy at least two. If you want to keep just one, go to a rescue centre, as they may have ferrets that prefer being on their own.

The jill on the left is smaller and a bit faster than the hob on the right.

HOB OR JILL?
Male ferrets are called hobs, females are called jills. Hobs are about twice the size of jills. Whichever you choose, it is best to keep **neutered** animals. After they have been neutered, hobs and jills can be kept together. Neutering can be done either with an operation or an injection. Ask your vet which they recommend for your ferret.

KITS

Ferrets give birth to between three and seven babies, which are called kits. It is vital for kits to stay with their mother for at least six weeks after they are born so that they develop properly. When they reach 8–10 weeks of age, they are ready to leave their mothers. If you choose young ferrets, make sure they are bright and alert, with a soft, clean coat and are willing to be handled by you.

These two 10-week-olds kits are ready to move to their new home.

STINK ALERT!

Ferrets naturally produce a distinctive smell through **scent glands**. Some people find the smell unpleasant, but neutering removes most of it. Don't feel tempted to wash their smell off them – that will only make it come back even more strongly. If frightened, your pet may let off a particularly nasty 'stink bomb', but this smell goes away quite quickly.

Ferrets of all ages will sleep together. Here, two youngsters are curled up between two adults.

WORKING FERRETS

Ferrets were first domesticated in ancient Egypt more than 2,000 years ago. The Egyptians probably used ferrets to catch rabbits. Today, working ferrets are still used by farmers to keep rabbit numbers down. This hunting method is known as ferreting.

This tapestry shows people hunting rabbits with ferrets in Scotland in the 15th century.

DOWN THE HOLE

To catch rabbits, ferreters take advantage of ferrets' natural instincts to chase through tunnels, which they have inherited from polecats. First, the ferreters cover the exits from a rabbit warren with nets. Next, they send the ferret down the warren, where it runs through the tunnels searching for rabbits. The rabbits in the warren smell the ferret and make a run for it. As they try to escape, they are caught in the nets.

WHY USE FERRETS?

You might think that ferreting is a cruel thing to do, but there are advantages to using ferrets to catch rabbits. Farmers need to control the numbers of rabbits on their farms as rabbits damage their crops. The alternative to using ferrets is to use poison, but using ferrets ensures that the farmers do not kill anything else. Ferrets only target rabbits, but poisons will also kill foxes, badgers and other animals.

After flushing the rabbits out of their warren, the ferret returns to the surface. The ferreters attach an electronic transmitter to the ferret so that they know exactly where to find it.

This ferret's jaws are smaller and weaker than those of a polecat.

SMALL JAWS

Ferrets would not survive for long in the wild. Their natural curiosity leads them down rabbit warrens, but their jaws are too weak for them to catch the rabbits. The wild polecat has a stronger jaw, which it can use to bite into a rabbit's neck and kill it.

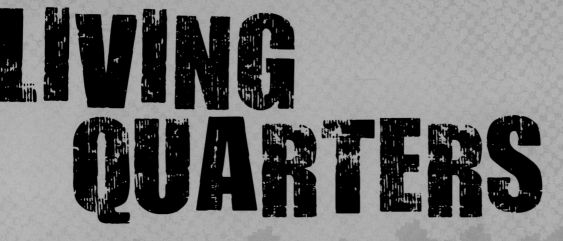

LIVING QUARTERS

Your ferrets will need a special enclosure to live in. You can buy metal cages or wooden hutches, or you can build your own. Ferrets can be kept inside or outside in a shed. Wherever you keep your ferrets, they will need plenty of space to play and explore.

A COMFY BED

Ferrets spend more than half their lives asleep, so they will need a comfortable bed. This should be a box or crate lined with blankets. They also love playing and sleeping in a **hammock**. You can make a hammock by hanging a pillowcase from the roof of the cage.

Your ferrets will take a snooze in a hammock, but you will need to give them a dark place to have longer sleeps.

This ferret lives in a wooden hutch in a garden shed. If keeping ferrets outside, you must make sure they do not get too cold in winter.

SEPARATE AREAS

The cage needs to have a separate area for sleeping and another for a toilet. A two-storey cage is ideal as it will give your ferret different spaces to explore. The ferrets will sleep upstairs but they will feed, play and go to the toilet downstairs. The cage should have a solid floor covered in a loose **substrate** of wood shavings or sawdust. Ferrets are very clean and always go to the toilet in the same place. They will choose the spot to use for their toilet themselves.

This ferret is kept indoors in a large cage. It has just eaten. Ferrets give their lips a thorough clean after eating.

BUILDING YOUR OWN HUTCH

Many ferret keepers build their own hutch in a garden shed. The advantage of doing this is that you can give your ferrets more space to play in. A home for a pair of ferrets should ideally be at least 1.5 metres long, but the more space you can give them the better.

WILD COUSINS

Comparing the habits of the wild polecat with those of ferrets helps us to understand why ferrets act the way they do. What a polecat does to survive, your ferret will do just for fun.

Polecats dig several tunnels, or burrows, in their territories.

BURROWERS

Polecats dig underground burrows to live in, which they keep clean and tidy. Ferrets like digging in anything soft and soil-like and exploring underground tunnels. They also make sure that they do not leave droppings anywhere near their sleeping areas.

FUSSY EATER

Polecat kits leave their mothers when they are about four months old. During their first four months, they learn from their mothers what food is good for them. As adults, they will catch for themselves the things that they were fed as youngsters. Ferrets also develop their tastes in their first few months, and it can be hard to make an adult try new things.

BORN HUNTER

Polecats have poor eyesight, but respond to movements that are about the speed of a small **rodent** running away from them, which they will pounce on. Ferrets show the same behaviour when they play. If you drag a toy along the floor at the speed of a fleeing mouse, your ferret will chase and 'kill' it.

Polecats have an excellent sense of smell and use it to track down **prey**. They use their eyes to hunt only once they are very close to their prey.

FOOD HOARDERS

When a polecat kills an animal that is too big to eat in one go, it drags its catch back to its home, where it will eat it in several separate meals. Ferrets often do the same thing with their food, and also collect any other small things that they find, such as your missing keys (but they won't try to eat your keys)!

GREAT MATES

When you get to know your ferrets, you will learn that they each have their own personalities. Some will be outgoing and noisy, while others may be quiet and shy. With regular human contact, even shy ferrets will soon come to trust you.

When you pick a ferret up, hold one hand behind its front legs and use the other hand to support its bottom.

14

BITING

Ferrets sometimes play rough and may give you a nip. Kits do this without realising that they are hurting you, and may break the skin. Be patient with them, and they will learn not to do it. When they are frightened, ferrets are capable of giving a sharp bite. When you get to know them, you will learn when it is best to leave them alone.

Ferrets sometimes play-fight with one another. This is normal, and they will be curled up asleep together an hour or two later.

SHARP BITE

If your ferret is frightened or hurt, it may give you a bite that is sharp enough to draw blood. If this happens, tell an adult. You should wash the bite and apply antibacterial cream to it. If the bite is really deep, you may need to go to the doctor, but very bad bites are rare.

HANDLING YOUR FERRET

Most ferrets are happy to be picked up, but don't try to hold on to a struggling animal. If the ferret has come from a rescue centre, it may be a little nervous. Give it time to get used to you – many rescued ferrets have been mistreated in the past and have bad memories of people.

This kit is just a couple of weeks old. It needs to be with its mother most of the time, but can be handled, too, and may fall asleep on you. Regular handling when very young gets ferrets used to human contact.

PLAYTIME

Your ferrets will spend most of their waking hours racing around and playing. They can play a little inside their cages, but you will also need to take them out for a run around every day.

OUTDOOR RUN

If you have a garden, it is a great idea to ask an adult to help you build a run for your ferrets so that they can play on their own. You can make a run out of a wooden frame with steel mesh stretched across it. Cover the floor with soil and provide a bedding area for the ferrets to take an occasional nap.

Use piping to build your ferrets tunnels to run through – it will be just like running down a rabbit hole.

WEASEL WAR DANCE

When it is particularly excited, a ferret may perform an energetic dance known as a weasel war dance. It will arch its back, hop sideways and backwards and dash around with its tail puffed up. You may think your ferret has gone totally crazy, but the weasel war dance is usually a sign that it is really enjoying itself. In the wild, polecats do this to confuse their prey.

Give your ferrets lots of toys to play with. They will pretend to hunt balls, pouncing on them as if they were prey.

FERRET-PROOF HOME

When you let your ferrets loose inside the house, you need to make sure that there is nothing sharp that they can injure themselves on, and nothing valuable that they could knock over. Ferrets can cause mayhem if left unsupervised, so make sure you watch them when they are out and about.

Show a bucket to a ferret and it will jump inside, and probably knock it over!

FEEDING TIME

Ferrets are **carnivores** and should only be fed meat-based food that is high in energy. You can buy dried ferret food that contains the **nutrients** and energy that ferrets need. Ferrets also like to eat fresh meat. A mix of fresh meat and dry food makes for a healthy diet.

FRESH WATER

It is essential for your ferrets to have access to fresh water all the time. Use a heavy water bowl that they will not be able to tip over, and change the water every day. This is particularly important in summer as ferrets can **dehydrate** very quickly.

DRY FOOD

Feed your ferrets dry food that is specially made for ferrets. You can buy this from a pet shop. Ferret food is high in protein, and also contains lots of fat, which the ferrets need to give them energy. Ferrets need to eat small amounts several times a day, so make sure they always have dry food available to them.

Leave out a bowl of dry food, which your ferrets will nibble on whenever they want.

FRESH MEAT

Fresh meat is good for ferrets. You can buy cheap cuts of meat such as heart, liver or kidneys from a butcher. They will also eat cooked chicken and white fish. Ferrets often hide food to eat later, so if you give them fresh meat, check their cages regularly for any old bits that have not been eaten.

Like polecats, ferrets have sharp teeth for stabbing and tearing at prey.

Give your ferrets raw pork bones – gnawing on bones keeps their teeth clean.

KEEPING ACTIVE

Ferrets become bored very easily. It is important to give them toys to play with and to allow them as much time as you can outside their cage to go exploring.

PLAYING OUTSIDE

Your ferrets will go wild when they see piles of dead leaves to play with in the autumn. In winter, they will love playing in the snow, but ferrets get cold quickly, so only allow them out for a few minutes. Ferrets also don't like extreme heat, so leave them inside in a cool place on hot summer days.

Ferrets have fun digging in snow.

GOING FOR WALKS

Some ferrets can be taken for walks on a **harness**. You will need to get your ferret used to wearing a harness inside first. When it is comfortable with the harness, you can venture outside. Limit walks to 20 minutes and always take water with you. Your ferret will expect you to go where it wants to go. It will feel like the ferret is taking you for a walk!

Not all ferrets like wearing a harness. If you have a ferret that struggles every time you try to put one on, it is best not to take it for walks.

Ferrets will investigate everything with their noses and mouths, so be careful what you leave lying around.

CHANGE THEIR TOYS

A ferret will play with almost anything: tubes, plastic bags or a pair of old boots! Try hanging a ball from the roof of your ferrets' cage. They will soon be leaping up trying to grab hold of it. Change the toys around regularly – like you, a ferret will become bored if it has the same toys all the time.

SHOWTIME!

Ferret clubs hold shows where you can enter your ferret in competitions. Shows are great places to meet fellow ferret lovers and their pets. Most clubs hold open shows, so you do not have to be a member to show your ferret.

WHAT CLASS IS YOUR FERRET?

Ferrets are grouped into different **classes** depending on the colour of their fur. Hobs and jills are judged separately. There may also be special classes for kits, veterans, disabled, rescue and working ferrets. Whatever the age, colour or size of your ferret, there will be a class for it.

JUDGING THE FERRETS

At the show, the judges are looking for a lively, friendly ferret that is the right colour for its class. They award points for personality as well as looks. At the end, an overall winner is chosen from all the classes, and named 'Best in Show'.

The ferrets don't care about the competition, but they do get to meet lots of other ferrets.

These ferrets are, from the left: sandy, polecat, albino and silver.

BATHTIME

Before a show, you will need to give your ferret a bath so that it looks its best. Use a special ferret shampoo, and avoid the face and eyes. Use lukewarm water and dip the ferret in it. Dry your ferret off with a towel, then allow it to dry itself completely by dashing around the room.

Do not cover the ferret completely in water.

23

ON YOUR MARKS!

Many ferret rescue centres organize ferret races at country shows and school fairs. For most people, this is the first time they have ever seen a ferret close-up. The rescue centres use the races to raise money for their work caring for abandoned ferrets.

You get to meet all the competitors between races.

OBSTACLE COURSE

A racetrack is made up of tubes connecting a series of boxes. One ferret is released into each tube, and they must make it all the way down to the end of the tracks before turning round and coming back. Along the way there are obstacles to negotiate, such as a water jump, a seesaw and a bridge.

RESCUE CENTRES

Sadly, many ferrets are abandoned every year. **Strays** are taken in by ferret rescue centres, which give them the medical care they need after living rough and find them new homes. Ferrets cannot survive for long in the wild, so the rescue centres save these ferrets' lives.

The ferrets that rescue centres take in are often in need of urgent medical attention. When they are ill, ferrets often lose their fur.

MINDS OF THEIR OWN

The watching crowd pick their favourite ferret and cheer it on. Many things can go wrong for your chosen ferret. Ferrets have a mind of their own, so they'll only race if they want to. They may stop to play on the seesaw, decide to back up the wrong way or just take a break half-way along the track!

The first ferret to appear back at the start of its tube is the winner.

STAYING HEALTHY

To keep your ferrets healthy, find a local vet who has experience looking after ferrets. You should also regularly check their bodies yourself to make sure they are staying healthy. Think about having your ferrets **microchipped** in case they get lost.

The vet will check that your ferret's teeth are strong and healthy.

THINGS TO LOOK FOR

- Check your ferrets' claws every few weeks. If they get too long, you will need to clip them with a pair of nail clippers.

- If your ferrets' eating or drinking habits change, see a vet straight away. This is often the first sign of illness.

- Ferrets can catch colds from humans, so make sure nobody with a cold handles them.

- Look for signs that your ferret might be feeling stressed. Signs include hiding, hissing or biting more than normal. A stressed ferret is much more likely to get ill.

- Watch for a ferret that is having difficulty moving. This is a sign that it is in pain and may have an injury.

- If their ears become dirty, carefully clean them with a cotton bud.

VACCINATION AND NEUTERING

If your ferrets have not been neutered, you will need to take them to the vet to have an operation or injection. Many vets recommend a 'jill jab' for females as an alternative to neutering. This is a yearly injection of **hormones** that stop jills from breeding. Ferrets also need to be **vaccinated** against a disease called canine distemper, which they can catch from dogs. This involves a yearly visit to the vet for an injection.

GOING AWAY

When you go away, you will need to leave your ferrets at a **boarding house**. Ferret clubs keep lists of boarding houses near you. You'll need an up-to-date vaccination certificate before your ferret is allowed in.

When transporting your ferret, you will need a pet carrier.

GROWING OLD

Ferrets live on average for 8–10 years, and you should have many happy years with your pets. However, when they reach about six years of age, they will start to slow down and sleep even more than they used to. Older ferrets may need special care and attention.

KEEPING A RECORD

A great way to remember your ferrets is to keep a scrapbook with photos and any prizes they won. You could also make a webpage and share your favourite images of your ferrets with your friends.

As ferrets age, their muscles become weaker. You may need to rearrange an old ferret's cage so that everything is on one level and within easy reach.

SAYING GOODBYE

At the end of its life, your old ferret might curl up and go to sleep peacefully. However, if your ferret becomes very ill, the kindest thing to do is to have it **put down**. You will feel sad when your pet dies, but in time the pain will pass and you will be left with happy memories of your time together.

AMAZING FERRET FACTS

A newborn ferret is small enough to fit inside a teaspoon. Ferrets are born deaf and blind.

All ferrets are white when they are born. They start to develop their adult colour after about three weeks.

The name 'ferret' comes from a **Latin** word meaning 'thief'.

A ferret's resting heart rate is about 220 beats per minute. That's three times faster than the average human heart rate.

Ferrets sleep for about 18 hours a day.

FERRET QUIZ

Test your ferret knowledge with this short quiz.

Can you name these different ferret colours?

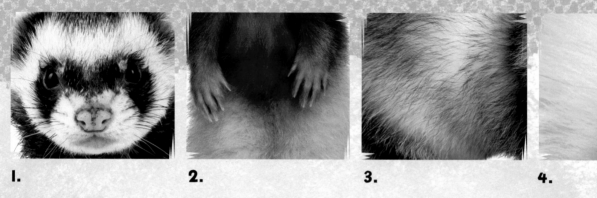

1.

2.

3.

4.

5. What is the name for a female ferret?

6. What wild animal is the ferret descended from?

7. How long should kits stay with their mothers?

8. How many hours do ferrets spend sleeping each day?

9. Why do ferrets need to be vaccinated?

10. What colour are kits when they are born?

ANSWERS
1. Polecat
2. Sandy
3. Silver
4. Albino
5. Jill
6. European polecat
7. At least six weeks
8. About 18 hours a day
9. To protect them from the disease canine distemper
10. White

GLOSSARY

ANTIBACTERIAL CREAM
A special cream that kills germs, which is rubbed on cuts to stop them from becoming infected.

BOARDING HOUSE
A place where pet owners leave their animals when they go away. The animals are properly cared for and kept safe.

BREEDER
A person who keeps animals to produce and sell the young.

CARNIVORE
An animal that hunts and eats other animals.

CLASSES
The different groups of ferret in shows. Ferrets fall into different classes according to the colour of their fur.

DEHYDRATE
When an animal loses so much water from its body that it becomes sick. Ferrets can dehydrate very easily in hot weather.

DESCENDED
Bred from particular ancestors. Ferrets are descended from the wild European polecat.

DOMESTICATED
Bred to live with humans. Domesticated animals would struggle to survive in the wild without human care.

HAMMOCK
A piece of cloth that is hung between two points and can be used to play or sleep on.

HARNESS
A collar that is attached to an animal so that it can be held on a lead when it goes for a walk.

HORMONE
A chemical produced by the body to control particular processes, such as breeding seasons.

LATIN
A language spoken in the ancient Roman Empire.

MAMMAL
A warm-blooded animal with fur or hair on its body that feeds its young with milk.

MICROCHIPPING
Fitting an electronic chip with information about the animal under an animal's skin. A microchipped animal that gets lost can be returned to its owner, whose address is on the chip.

NEUTERING
Giving an operation that stops an animal from breeding.

NUTRIENTS
Chemical substances contained in food that the body needs to stay healthy. Ferrets need a high-protein, high-fat diet to give them the nutrients they need.

PREY
An animal that is hunted and killed by other animals for food.

PUT DOWN
To end the life of a sick animal with an injection that peacefully puts it to sleep so that it then dies.

RODENT
A type of mammal that has four large front teeth that keep growing throughout its life. Polecats hunt rodents such as rabbits.

SCENT GLAND
A body part that produces a particular smell. Ferrets have scent glands near their bottoms that can produce a very powerful stink to scare off attackers.

STRAY
A pet animal that has been abandoned by its owner or has become lost and is living in the streets or in the wild. Stray ferrets struggle to survive without human care.

SUBSTRATE
Loose material such as wood shavings that is placed at the bottom of a ferret's cage. The substrate should be changed regularly.

VACCINATED
Given medicine that protects against certain diseases.

USEFUL WEBSITES

www.nfws.net
Website of the National Ferret Welfare Society, with information on all aspects of ferret care and information about ferret vets, working ferrets and shows.

www.rspca.org.uk
Website of the Royal Society for the Prevention of Cruelty to Animals, with advice and information about caring for all kinds of pets, including ferrets.

INDEX

the PET -to- GET

Is a ferret for you?
Choosing your ferret
Working ferrets
Living quarters
Wild cousins
Making friends
Playtime
Feeding your ferret
Keeping active
Showtime
On your marks!
Staying healthy
Growing old
Ferret quiz

978 0 7502 8292 5

Is a lizard for you?
Which lizard?
Bearded dragon
Home sweet home
Hide & seek
Leopard gecko
Dinner time
Savannah monitor
Lizard mates
Panther chameleon
Health check
Green iguana
Saying goodbye
Lizard quiz

978 0 7502 8288 8

Why a rat?
The right rat
Rats in the wild
Fancy rats
Moving in
Playtime
Dinner time
Great mates
Out and about
Health check
At the vet
Rat shows
Growing old
Rat quiz

978 0 7502 8289 5

Why a snake?
Which snake?
Corn snake
Snake house
Clean and healthy
Grey rat snake
Dinner time
Garter snake
Out and about
Ball python
Health check
Milk snake
Growing old
Snake quiz

978 0 7502 8290 1

Why a spider?
Which spider?
Spiders in the wild
A safe place
Chilean rose tarantula
Feeding your spider
Mexican red tarantula
Close encounters
The moult
Costa Rican zebra
Breeding spiders
Mexican blonde tarantula
Spider first aid
Spider quiz

978 0 7502 8291 8

WAYLAND